Wacky World of...

Baffling Buildings!

by Hermione Redshaw

BEARPORT
PUBLISHING

Minneapolis, Minnesota

CREDITS

All images are courtesy of Shutterstock.com, unless otherwise specified. With thanks to Getty Images, Thinkstock Photo, and iStockphoto.

Recurring assets – Lelene (header font), MaryMB (explosion), RoyaltyFreeStockVectors (spiral), Ardea, hvostik (series logo), Amy Li (additional illustrations). Cover – Teo Stuivenberg, Anna Jastrzebska, p2–3 – Gulcin Ragiboglu, p4–5 – Alexander Konradi, Ian Knox (wiki commons), karelnoppe, Uwe Aranas, Oliverouge 3. p6–7 – dnaveh, Jaguar PS, p8–9 – Barna Tanko, Nowaczyk, p10–11 – Mehmet Hilmi Barcin, Nadzin, Syda Productions, TashaNatasha, p12–13 – Archi0780, p14–15 – Guenter Albers, Chipdawes (wiki commons), p16–17 – TashaNatasha, tsuneomp, unknown (wiki commons), p18–19 – pisaphotography, iVazoUSky, p20–21 – Taras Grebinets, Basileus, Matauw, Dragon Images, dordek, p22–23 – saiko3p, CJM Grafx, katatonia82, Just dance.

Library of Congress Cataloging-in-Publication Data is available at www.loc.gov or upon request from the publisher.

ISBN: 979-8-88509-381-1 (hardcover)
ISBN: 979-8-88509-503-7 (paperback)
ISBN: 979-8-88509-618-8 (ebook)

© 2023 Booklife Publishing
This edition is published by arrangement with Booklife Publishing.

North American adaptations © 2023 Bearport Publishing Company. All rights reserved. No part of this publication may be reproduced in whole or in part, stored in any retrieval system, or transmitted in any form or by any means, electronic, mechanical, photocopying, recording, or otherwise, without written permission from the publisher.

For more information, write to Bearport Publishing, 5357 Penn Avenue South, Minneapolis, MN 55419.

CONTENTS

BUILDINGS 4
THE DANCING HOUSE 6
CASA TERRACOTA 8
MODELING HOUSES 10
EARTH HOUSES 12
THE PYRAMIDS 14
WHAT LIES INSIDE? 16
THE LEANING TOWER OF PISA . . 18
BUILD IT! 20
BARELY BAFFLING 22
GLOSSARY 24
INDEX 24

BUILDINGS

There is no doubt that humans do some very strange things. We turn vegetables into batteries and make art out of grass. We even remake volcanoes for fun . . . and we don't stop there!

When it comes to the places where we eat, sleep, and work, we have built things that are quite **baffling**. Some buildings are huge. Others are crazy shapes. And then there are the buildings that just don't make sense.

THE DANCING HOUSE
CZECH REPUBLIC

This building has moves! It was **designed** by Vlado Milunić and Frank Gehry to represent the shape of famous dancing couple, Fred Astaire and Ginger Rogers. Because of this, the building is sometimes known as Fred and Ginger.

The real Fred and Ginger were movie stars from the 1930s and 1940s.

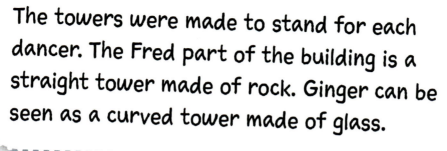

The towers were made to stand for each dancer. The Fred part of the building is a straight tower made of rock. Ginger can be seen as a curved tower made of glass.

The Dancing House is currently a hotel.

CASA TERRACOTA
COLOMBIA

A red rock building in the mountains of Colombia baffles visitors. The Casa Terracota was built entirely out of clay found nearby. The handmade structure was **sculpted** by a man named Octavio Mendoza Morales. It is known for its unique color, shape, and style.

THE FANTASTIC BUILDING HIDES SOME SURPRISES INSIDE, INCLUDING A GIANT SPIDER!

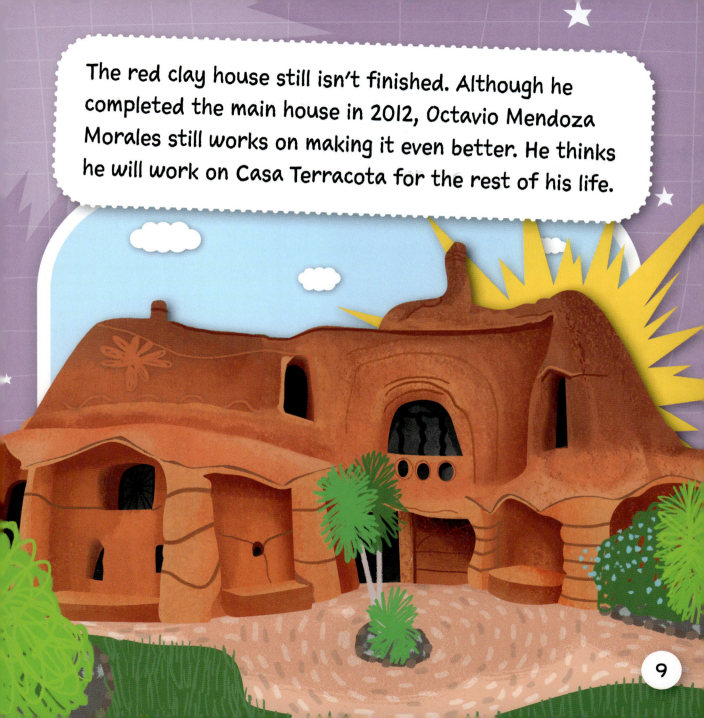

The red clay house still isn't finished. Although he completed the main house in 2012, Octavio Mendoza Morales still works on making it even better. He thinks he will work on Casa Terracota for the rest of his life.

MODELING HOUSES

The clay Mendoza uses to build his house is soft when it is wet. Then, it dries in the sun and becomes hard. This is a lot like modeling clay you may have used for art projects.

Try building your own model clay house.

Will you make a big or small house?

What kind of person lives in your house?

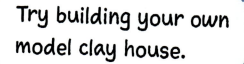

How many rooms will you make?

Is there anything wacky about your house?

Will it have straight or curved walls?

Remember, no design is too wild!

EARTH HOUSES
SWITZERLAND

Mendoza isn't the only creator who made a building that blends in. Travel to Switzerland and you'll see nine houses that are actually built into the ground. Their tops are covered in grass.

THE PYRAMIDS
EGYPT

Some buildings are meant to stand out. Ancient Egyptians built the pyramids as places to bury their **pharaohs.** Each pyramid's size was meant to show the importance of the person it was made for.

The tallest pyramid is the Great Pyramid of Giza. It belonged to Pharaoh Khufu.

It's still not clear how the pyramids were built. Ancient Egyptians did not have the tools we have today, but the pyramids have lasted for more than 4,000 years.

SOME PEOPLE SAY THE EGYPTIANS USED THE STARS TO LINE UP THE CORNERS OF THE PYRAMID PERFECTLY NORTH, SOUTH, WEST, AND EAST.

WHAT LIES INSIDE?

A pyramid can have many rooms inside. Every pyramid has at least a room where the pharaoh was buried. Sometimes, there are also rooms for a pharaoh's **treasures**. The ancient Egyptians believed you could carry riches into the **afterlife**.

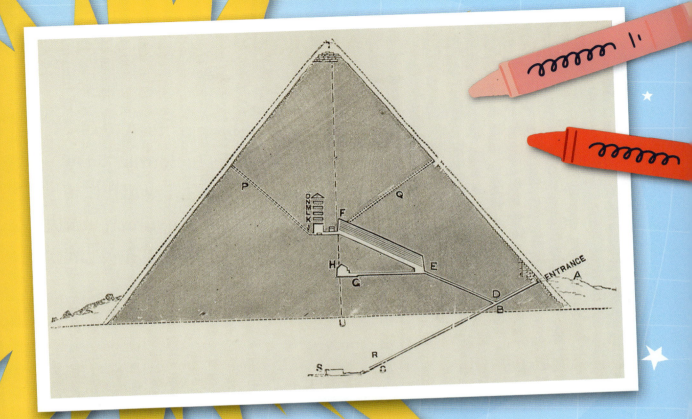

How would you design the inside of a pyramid with different rooms and passages? Think about how many rooms to make and what kinds of treasures you might want with you if you were a pharaoh.

THE LEANING TOWER OF PISA

ITALY

The Tower of Pisa wasn't meant to be leaning. The ground underneath it is soft in spots, which made part of the building sink.

The tower started leaning before it was even finished being built.

People have tried to straighten the Leaning Tower of Pisa in different ways. Some tried adding extra cement to the building's **foundation** to keep it from falling over. One wacky suggestion was to take it apart stone by stone and rebuild it somewhere else.

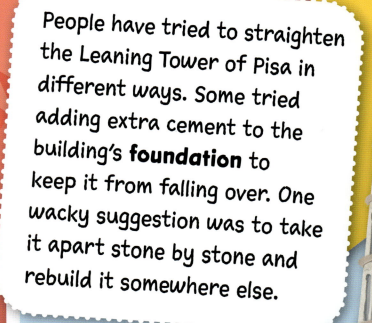

BUILD IT!

Make your own baffling building. How high can you build and have your structure stay standing?

What will you use to build? Heavy objects are stronger, but they are more likely to fall when stacked strangely. Lighter things may be easier to use to create crazy shapes, but they are less steady high up.

20

Here are some ways to keep a baffling building standing!

WIDER BOTTOM

Using a solid base will help if you want to build tall.

ZIGZAG

Build up one direction and then another.

BALANCE

Make sure your building is balanced on either side.

BARELY BAFFLING

Check out even more crazy buildings!

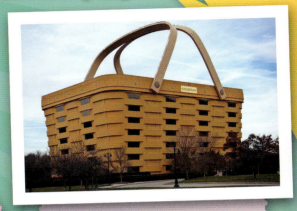

HANG NGA GUESTHOUSE
- Found in Vietnam
- Built in 1990
- Is a large hotel

THE BIG BASKET BUILDING
- Found in Ohio
- Built in 1997
- Was originally an office building for a basket company

KRZYWY DOMEK
- Found in Poland
- Built in 2004
- Is part of a shopping center

GLOSSARY

afterlife the life of a person after they die

baffling extremely confusing or hard to understand

designed thought up, planned, or created

foundation a base made of stone, concrete, or other material that supports a building from underneath

pharaohs ancient Egyptian kings

sculpted made into a shape

treasures objects of value that are hidden or kept in a safe place

INDEX

ancient Egypt 14–16
clay 8–11
design 6, 11, 13, 17

Earth houses 12–13
eco-friendly 13
leaning 18–19

sculpt 8
towers 7, 18–19